Made in United States
Orlando, FL
15 April 2025

60550071R00057